YOU & YOUR
BODY

YOU & YOUR
BODY

WHAT IF YOUR BODY ISN'T A PROBLEM?

KALPANA RAGHURAMAN
EDITED BY MONICA GILLIAM

AC PUBLISHING

You & Your Body
Copyright © 2024 by Kalpana Raghuraman
Cover Design: Sandra Schoenmakers

ISBN: 978-1-63493-655-2 (paperback)
ISBN: 978-1-63493-656-9 (ebook)

All rights reserved. No part of this publication may bere produced, stored in a retrieval system, or transmitted, in any form or by any means electronic, mechanical, photocopying, recording, or otherwise without prior written permission from the publisher.

The author and publisher of the book do not make any claim or guarantee for any physical, mental, emotional, spiritual, or financial result. All products, services and information provided by the author are for general education and entertainment purposes only. The information provided herein is in no way a substitute for medical advice. In the event you use any of the information contained in this book for yourself, the author and publisher assume no responsibility for your actions.

Published by Access Consciousness® Publishing
www.acpublishing.com

Second Edition

First Edition, copyright © 2020 by Kalpana Raghuraman, published by Big Moose Publishing

This book is dedicated to all of our bodies
May we step ever further into the gifts that they are

Contents

Acknowledgments..i
Introduction..iii
Listen to Your Body...1
Does Your Body Make You Right or Wrong?...........................8
Choosing to Create Your Body.....................................14
Creating Your Body With Judgment.................................22
What Are You Eating?...30
Don't Freak Out! It's Just Awareness.............................36
Fitting In...38
How Are You Using Your Weight?...................................44
The Mirror...51
Who Are You Creating Your Body For?..............................60
Hiding...65
Does Your Body Need to Change?...................................71
Living or Dying..74
Now What?..78
Wanting More?..80
About the Author...82

At the end of the day, it is the body that gives us access to tasting and receiving the joy of living. So let's have it, shall we?!

Acknowledgments

I would like to start with a moment of gratitude for all the people who made this book possible.

First of all, a big thank you to the wonderful Monica Gilliam. With her magical touch she brought all the content together and edited this book from front to back and turned it into what it is today.

Next, I'd like to thank the lovely Fay Thompson. For her kindness and guidance in the creation of my very first book. She made it possible for this book to come to life.

And then on to Sandra Schoenmakers. She was the one creating the beautiful artwork for this book and coordinating the creation. She has also been a part of the editing process as well as the book translations. A big thank you to her and her ongoing support.

Freeke Joan has also been a great contribution. She was also part of the editing process as well as an ongoing support. A big thank you to her, her sharpness and lightness.

Last but absolutely not the least: my deep gratitude goes to Gary Douglas and Dr. Dain Heer. For their ongoing support and inspiration and for the immense wealth that Access Consciousness is to the world and to myself. Thank you, thank you!

I consider myself blessed to be surrounded by such brilliant people. I am proud of how "You & your Body" turned out. I hope it will contribute to many people all over the world.

Making their body a friend....

Introduction

Did you know that your body can directly give you information about what works for it?

Have you ever taken a moment to ask your body what it would like?

What clothes would it like to wear?

What food would it like to eat?

What people would it like to hug?

For some of you, this may be an incredibly different way of approaching your body.

Others may think it's just nuts.

But really, would it hurt to try it out?

After all, your stomach tells you when it is hungry, and your back tells you when it is uncomfortable. Why not cultivate your skills in talking with your body?

What if the journey to creating a joyful, thriving body could be led by the simple, yet world changing tool of asking questions?

Contrary to how you may have been taught to interact with a question, the key is not to focus on any particular answer, but rather, to acknowledge all of the different responses that arise. When you ask a question, all sorts of information becomes available to you. Some of this information may be cognitive; as in, you may ask a question and have words or thoughts come to mind. Sometimes though, the responses to the questions you ask come as more of an energetic awareness. This energetic awareness may show up as sensations in the body, or other kinds of "feelings". When you start to notice all of these sensations and information, you may be surprised to discover how much more clarity you can have in your daily life. All of this information is simply, in essence, awareness.

Your awareness is the golden treasure that can assist you to create a life and body you enjoy. Like a child exploring the world with "What is this?", "Where did that come from?", and "How does that work?", questions can become your allies in exploring the world around you. When you approach a question with curiosity, you may be surprised at all that you discover, beyond anything you have previously decided or concluded.

Decisions, definitions, and conclusions simply put an end to the journey of change and discovery that is possible. When you ask a question and look for a specific, "correct" answer, more often than not, you begin to exclude all kinds of information from even entering your awareness.

Answers are the conclusions we come to that filter out anything that does not match what we have decided is so. For example, if you have decided that the answer to changing your weight lies in your diet, you may overlook the impact that your relationships are having on your body.

This book will provide you with many questions to ask yourself and your body. The purpose of these questions is for you to gain more awareness about where you are functioning from. Sometimes you may discover that you are basing your choices with your body and your life on a point of view from your childhood - a point of view that could possibly use an update!

You are more than welcome to let go of any of the

ideas that you have been using to create your life (and your body) thus far. In fact, why not try that now?

Are there any points of view that you have been holding onto about your body that are not adding to the joy of your life? What are the big ones that come up right away? Would you be willing to simply choose to let them go?

Watch out. It may be MUCH easier than you would imagine.

Listen to Your Body

"The body is this organism that we create to create awareness, and few of us use it as that. Rather than seeing the gift of awareness that it gives us, we keep trying to choose something that will eliminate that.

What if you were willing to see the gift your body is to you instead of seeing the detriment it is to you?"

- Gary Douglas, Founder of Access Consciousness®

Take a moment to imagine your life without the sense of touch.

How would that be for you?

How about if you had no sense of taste, or smell,

motion, sight, or sound?

Do you ever stop to thank your body for all that it is contributing to your life? Or do you simply notice when something is not how you would like it to be?

As you start to actually acknowledge the immense awareness that your body is being and gifting to you all the time, more than you might even imagine can begin to change. After all, you are living with and through this body of yours. Are you willing to actually enjoy your body and the vast presence and knowing that it brings? Or, are you committed to struggling against the awareness that your body offers, as though your body is your enemy?

Unfortunately, many of us have learned to vilify and pathologize our awareness and especially the awareness that comes from our bodies rather than use all this awareness to create lives that we enjoy. We have been like Chicken Little, crying that the sky is falling any time something drops on our heads.

Would you be willing to let go of the idea that every little thing you're aware of has to do with you specifically? Yes, even when it comes to your body. Newsflash: not every sensation your body alerts you to has to do with your body. And you don't always require to change what is going on with your body to shift those sensations.

Say, for instance, you are chatting with someone who has really bad breath. Your nose gives you that information. In fact, your nose is probably picking up on and responding to a dizzying amount of information through scent alone. Though you are aware of the smell, it doesn't really have anything to do with you. Brushing your teeth would have no impact on their breath. But, noticing that they have breath that is not pleasant to you can actually open up different choices for you. You may choose to stand a little further away, or say no thank you to that make out session they are so interested in.

Whatever you choose to do with your awareness is part of the creation of the joyful adventure that living can be. Yet, when it comes to the body, many people often do not actually listen; and so they misidentify and misapply what their awareness is. Again, with the example of the bad breath, if you thought someone else's bad breath was yours, you could brush your teeth all day with no change in the smell. How frustrating would that be? If that were you, would you get upset with your body at all?

I wonder what you would do? Would you go to the dentist, or stop talking to other people? Would you convince yourself that you definitely have bad breath, that you only notice sometimes (like when that friend is around), but you're certain is there all the time?

This example may seem silly, but these are the crazy things we can do! All too often, when we are aware of something that we don't immediately like, we try to make it go away. We judge what our awareness is showing us and become fixated on stopping or changing the symptoms of our awareness.

And yet, if we look at our body as an organism of awareness, what possibilities open up? What can we start to allow as awareness through the body?

Body, what do you have to say?

Body, what do you have to say

QUESTIONS TO PLAY WITH

What do you know?
What would you like to choose?

How much energy have you been using to attempt to NOT be aware of what your body is showing you?

Have you used your body as proof of your wrongness or its wrongness when it is simply giving you awareness?

Where have you been diminishing, resisting, rejecting, or dismissing your awareness?

What if you could actually start to let your awareness flow through your body and your world with much more ease?

What if you could start to receive it all, without making it a problem?

What becomes available if you get out of this problem-fixing, result-oriented way of being with your body?

What if, as you acknowledge the awareness organism that your body is, the joy of embodiment can become a reality for you?

Does Your Body Make You Right or Wrong?

What does being right have to do with your body?

What is the right weight, size, or shape for you?

Who determines that?

We are, each of us, incredibly different. What if the standards that we are presented with do not really apply to our individual, unique bodies? The bulk of these standards, by the way, come from averages calculated by gathering data from a large group of individuals. We are then given these averages as though they apply to us individually. What a funny way to go about determining the direction that we, as individuals, should head towards.

Have any of you turned "the right weight" or "the right body shape and size" into a destination, as though once you reach that destination, YOU will finally be right? What have you decided that you have to have as a weight? And, what if that is not a constant?

I have chubby moments. I have a bit of a chubby moment going on right now. I'm like, "Okay. We're a bit chubby." It's nice and squooshy. And it's definitely more fun to hug me now. Some moments I am skinnier. I am not looking at it as a fixed thing. There is not a specific weight that I need to be that will then allow me to be happy, or that is the right weight.

What if there is no right weight for you either?

What if you could simply choose to let this particular point of view begin to shift, and let go of any specific weight as a destination?

So many of us have, quite simply, been sold fantasies about "rightness". We have been taught to strive for the right hair, the right clothes, the right husband, the right girlfriend, the right shoes, the right car, and the right weight. What if you could simply loosen the stranglehold that this notion of rightness has on you, on your life, and on the body you can create? How much have you been brainwashed to believe that you must have the right weight to be right, and if you have the wrong weight, then you would be wrong?

Would you be willing, for even one moment, to let go of the notion that there is a right weight, size, or shape for you and that you have to do everything you can to get to that "right" result?

Would you be willing to let go of everywhere that you have learned that your happiness is in any way dependent on you achieving the right body? While you're at it, would you be willing to let go of the supposed "wrongness" of your body as well?

At the core of right and wrong lies judgment. Rightness and wrongness always lead you back to judgment. The world we have grown up in continuously directs us to find more and more ways to judge, both ourselves and each other. If you take a moment to acknowledge the judgments that are all around you, you might be surprised at just how far they go. From your house to your education, to your career, to your holiday gifts, there is the chance to judge every single thing you choose. This entire world is based on being right and avoiding being wrong.

What if you could move away from rightness and wrongness and into the joy, possibilities, and choices that are available for you with your body including your weight, your body form, and your body shape?

QUESTIONS TO PLAY WITH

What do you know?
What would you like to choose?

Take a moment and ask yourself:

Where have I learned or decided that a certain weight, shape, or size is the right way to be?

What opinions and judgments do I have about any weight, shape, or size that is more or less than what I have defined as the "right" way to be?

Am I avoiding being wrong by having the "right" weight, shape, or size?

What weight, shape, or size would my body enjoy?

Are there any other ways that I am using my body to determine how I am right or wrong?

What does labeling my body as right or wrong give me?

Would I like to change any part of the right and wrong story I have been creating (or buying from others) with my body?

Choosing to Create Your Body

Each and every one of your choices is creative. These choices create in ways that may go beyond comprehension, but can definitely be observed. Sometimes you may make choices that create a big mess for you to clean up. And, sometimes you may make choices that create a nurturing space for you to enjoy.

Simple examples of this may be the choice to NOT look if there are cars coming as you cross the street, or the choice to eat some food that smells a little strange from your refrigerator. Many different outcomes are possible with each of these examples. After all, you can choose and choose again in each instant. You can choose to jump out of the way before that quiet car comes whizzing by. Or, you may choose to spit out that weird, leftover salad rather than spend a long, sick night wishing you had.

Whatever choices you make create the direction you are heading towards. Your choices set the stage for the future you will walk into. Some of the choices you make may not seem so obvious. You may not even realize when or how you are making some choices that have a large impact on what you are creating as your life. For example, you may choose to adopt an energy that is similar to your friends' and family's. After all, fitting in or "behaving appropriately" is both encouraged and, at times, even enforced in our world. Yet, no matter the circumstances, you are still the one in charge of making the choices that you make.

Though they may not be as immediately obvious, energetic choices are also creative. Take a moment and reflect on your life. Would you be willing to be vulnerable and honest with yourself, and to recognize the choices you have made that have created both the parts of your life that are working and the parts of your life that are more difficult? If you were to actually know that each and every choice you make is creating your life, would you make the same choices you are making now?

But wait, isn't this book about bodies? How does the creative power of our choices apply to our bodies? Well, many of us feel that our bodies are a little bit of a condemnation or a punishment - a thing we just have to deal with.

What if that is not the case?

What if you actually chose the creation of your body?

What if you chose who would be your father and who would be your mother, knowing that the synergy of their bodies coming together would create exactly this body that you have?

If you, for a moment, acknowledged even the possibility of that, would it in any way change the sense of being a victim to the creation of your body?

If you chose to come from the position of "I created this body", would you be able to come out of the fight with it and actually have fun with it?

Body, what are you capable of?

QUESTIONS TO PLAY WITH

What do you know?
What would you like to choose?

There are many everyday choices we make that create our bodies and shape the journeys we have with our bodies.

Ask yourself:

What thoughts am I using to create my body?

What emotions am I using to create my body?

What feelings am I using to create my body?

Who am I looking at as a model for how to create my body?

Am I copying and mimicking others to create my body?

Where can you have more presence, clarity, and choice with all of that? What if you were to create a body that matches who you are? A body that is not so much connected to other people and what they have determined is valuable, but rather, one that is connected to you and what you would like to explore with it?

Are you responding to your body as though it is just the result of everything that surrounds you? What if you start to have your body as a partner, a co-creator, where you engage your superpower of choice in its creation? Would you be willing to include your body in its own creation by asking more questions?

Some questions you can ask your body are:

Hey body, how would you like to look?

What can we create together?

What would you like to eat?

Where would you like to live?

What would you like to wear?

Who would you like to play with?

How would you like to move?

What are the possibilities for embodiment that I have not yet been exploring?

Use the information that you receive from these

questions to choose. Be present with what you would actually like to create. Make new choices, if you would like to. Then, enjoy the journey as your choices guide your creation. After all, if things are not heading in a direction that you like, you can always choose something else!

What can you choose, today and every day, that would allow your body to be everything it desires right away?

Creating Your Body with Judgment

What would it be like if you were to let go of all of the judgments you have of your body? Can you even imagine that? Is it possible that you could simply choose not to judge your body anymore? I mean, what does all of that judgment create anyway? Do the judgments you currently have of your body bring a smile to your face? Do they show you what a glorious gift it is to be alive? What role does judging your body play in your life?

You may be someone whose days are filled with the chatter of "My pants are too tight!" or "My weight is 69 kilos when really it should be 62." You may have all sorts of opinions about the different parts of your body, including their shapes and the ways those parts move. You are not alone.

The thing with this world is that we've been, unfortunately, quite brainwashed into thinking that we must judge our bodies. After all, everyone does it. We tell jokes about our bodies. We gossip about our bodies. We complain to our doctors and friends about our bodies.

We have not learned that we can actually be happy with our bodies. We have learned that there is always something better, and that is what we have to go for. We have learned to reject what we have and always look for what is outside, what is supposed to be better, what is supposed to be the right thing, and what is supposed to be "the thing".

Have you learned that you can change something through judgments? So often, people function from the point of view of "I don't like it. I have to judge it.", as if that judgment will change something. I mean, if you look at your nose and say, "Oh, it's so sharp. It's so ugly.", does it change? No. It makes it even more of that. It creates the energy that exaggerates and intensifies exactly what you have been judging. Judgment simply creates more judgment; it does not create change.

Judgment is the knife people use to cut themselves up, to destroy themselves, their bodies, their beauty, and their capacities. Are you willing to see what judgment is creating in your world? At the end of the day, you are the one choosing to judge whatever you choose to judge. And you are the only one who can stop the judgment you perpetrate on yourself.

You may be wondering, "Where does all this judgment come from?" Well, there are all the projections and definitions that people throw at us and that we see around us. We use these external points of view as reference points for how we should be and what our bodies should look like. We then turn those reference points into the standards that fuel our judgments.

How much have people been projecting at you that you're too fat, or you're too skinny, or too tall, too short, too this, too that? I know many people whose mothers would project on them things like, "You're so fat. I wish you were skinnier." Or, "Oh, I'm so pretty. Why are you so ugly?" Or, "You look just like your dad. I love him. But, dude, he's ugly."

When our mothers, our friends, and our entire world send us these messages, is it any wonder that we develop judgment and discomfort with our bodies? What if it didn't have to be this way for you? What if you didn't have to do what everybody else is doing with their bodies?

Allow yourself to be clear on what you are putting out there in your world about your body. Where are you loading your body with all of the energies of what you do not desire, as though that will change it into something else. Are you willing to look at that? Not from any judgment of what you have been doing, but more from, "Oh, going about it in that way isn't changing anything. What can I choose now?" Are there any projections you have been aware of that you have made more true than your choices?

And speaking of projections, how much of what has been projected at you and your body as the right and wrong ways to be is simply the points of view and judgments that people have about themselves and their own bodies? Where did they get those points of view and judgments from? Could it be that we have all been passing around points of view that we have bought from others without ever taking a moment to look at what we have been carrying?

What if all of it is just made up? How much effort have you put into matching the "rights" and "wrongs" everyone else is inventing? Would you be willing to let any or all of that go?

Right now.

Simply let it go.

Does that sound too easy?

What if it actually could be?

What if, rather than holding onto other people's points of view, you could begin to create your own way with your body - a way that works for you and changes as you and your body change? Would you be courageous enough to let go of the definitions about your body that you have bought, sold, invented, and been holding onto? By definitions, I mean the ideals that we strive to achieve, and the not-so-ideals that we strive to avoid.

Truly, how much have we been looking outside of ourselves, looking at other people, other bodies, and other choices to know what we can choose with our body, what we have to be with our body, and what we must have with our body? Will you give yourself the choice and the possibility to let go of all of that and allow your body to be and become the body that it truly is, without the judgments, definitions, and projections?

After all, your body is YOUR body, your gift of embodiment to play with as you move through the world. Or, have you given your body over to the world, to tell you if it's right or if it's wrong? For those of you who have done that, what would it be like if you didn't have to anymore? What if there is no "right" weight, no "right" shape, no "right" size? What if there is only what works for you and your body, and you get to go on the adventure of discovering what that is in every moment?

And so, what if you could basically reclaim your body again? Instead of letting other people tell you how you should cut your hair, YOU choose your haircut. And in a way, your body chooses it!

Are you willing to be different in a way where you stop judging your body?

Are you willing to stop telling your body exactly what you don't desire it to be?

Are you willing to stop using the judgments you are aware of as though they are the truth about you?

Are you willing to have the ease, the joy, the glory, the space, and the peace of not having to judge yourself into something you are not, and to no longer have a destination that you must reach?

QUESTIONS TO PLAY WITH

What do you know?
What would you like to choose?

Take a moment and ask yourself:

What definitions do I have of my body?

What definitions of my body am I using to always compare it to the bodies of other people?

Are there any definitions of my body I am using to have something to hate, to detest, to reject, and to judge about me?

Are there any definitions of my body I am using to continuously make my body and me wrong?

Be aware of everything that comes up and make the choice to let it all go if you would like to.

What Are You Eating?

What have you learned about food? And where have you learned all that you now consider to be true about food? Was it from your mom, your neighbour, your teacher, or even that latest fashion magazine? Where did all these sources get their information?

Have you ever tried to follow a particular diet? What was that like? Did you discover new foods and flavours that delighted your body? Did you force yourself to eat foods that tasted gross to you? Did you eat more or less than you wanted to?

These days there are a staggering amount of philosophies and points of view about what, when, how, where, and why to eat. Unfortunately, what one person suggests about food one day can be contradicted by someone else the next. What do you do when there is so much information to choose from? How do you discover what will work for you?

What if you were to simply start from where you are? When you are eating, allow yourself to get clear on what is going on for you, both physically and energetically. Ask your body what foods it would like, how much food it would like, and when. Begin to make the choices that work for both you and your body, free from the right and wrong of what might work for anyone else's body.

Please know that this will be an ongoing exploration. What your body might be hungry for one day may change the next. It is up to you to grow your presence with your body, to discover in each moment what will create the body and life that are vibrantly joyful... for you.

Please use the following section as a starting point for getting more clarity on how you are interacting with food and with eating. Dive into your curiosity. Ask yourself any and all questions that open up your awareness. Remember, this is an area where many people struggle and judge themselves. What if you could be different? What if you could simply choose, at the very least, to let go of any and all judgments you have around food and eating?

What if you were to begin to ask your body what it would like to eat and notice how it responds? This is an area where we can be very tricky with ourselves. Sometimes we may have subtle points of view that we use to skew or to direct the information we say we are getting from our bodies. Not to worry! Just keep asking questions and avoid coming to conclusions.

Continuously asking questions is a practice that can be quite different for each of us. The more questions you ask, the more awareness you get... even around asking questions. Just keep at it and allow yourself to have fun.

There is no need to judge yourself. You are an explorer. And now, you are exploring your body and the flavourful world of food.

Food is just food. It is not a villain or a saint.

In each moment you can ask, "Is this food going to be a gift to me and my body, or not? Is this food what my body requires and desires, or not?"

In short, ask your body. Have no point of view about what it says. It may surprise you! Have fun with the surprise.

QUESTIONS TO PLAY WITH

What do you know?
What would you like to choose?

Allow yourself to notice:

What are your habits and opinions about eating?

What do you choose to eat?

Do you ask your body what it would like to eat?

When do you choose to eat?

Do you always eat at the same time whether you are hungry or not?

Do you eat when you're bored? When you're emotional? When you are aware of something you'd rather avoid?

Do you eat to be social?

What choices are available for you around food and eating that you may not have been acknowledging?

Don't Freak Out! It's Just Awareness

When you start to ask questions, you may get much more awareness about all sorts of things.

Don't freak out! It's just awareness. It doesn't mean any particular thing. You do not have to do any set actions with your awareness. You can simply make choices with more information. And, you can choose anything! Even your choices will give you more awareness. None of your choices need to be set in stone. You have the privilege of choosing and choosing and choosing again.

If, as you begin to ask more of the questions in this book, you have the sense that more judgments about your body and your weight are coming up, you could ask if you are becoming more aware of the judgments that other people have about their own bodies.

How many people around you right now are judging the ways their bodies are showing up? Is it possible for you to be aware of everyone's judgments, even your own, and simply see that as information?

What if you could be aware of where others are functioning from without having to function in those same ways yourself? All of these things that are judgments, are they really real or are they just somebody's points of view that you are aware of?

What choices are available to you as you become more and more aware?

Fitting In

If you were to be totally you with no filters, no rules, no effort, no concerns, would you fit in? How different are you, really, than the people around you? How different are you than your family, your friends, and your peers?

How much have you moulded yourself to be like others so that you can fit in? Have you been measuring yourself against the people around you? What do measurements and comparisons actually give you? What if, after all, you were comparing apples to oranges? Yes, they are both fruits, but their flavours are very different!

Let's face it, even if we were to compare one apple with another apple, differences could be found. Yet, each apple is indeed an apple. Each apple is a fruit from the flowering of the apple tree. Each apple is succeeding at being an apple. It is only through judgments based on particular points of view that we would begin to say that one apple is better or worse than another. Each apple is an expression of the vitality of the earth and the tree it comes from, a gift that can feed the world in many ways.

What about your body? What gift is your body to the world? Have you ever really stopped to receive the gift of your body? Or have you gotten lost in comparing, competing, measuring, and judging your body in an effort to have that illusive "perfect" body?

What lies of "perfection" have you been using to determine whether or not you fit into the norms and ideals of this world? If you would not have those lies of perfection to measure yourself against, what could you create with your body? If you were to no longer buy into perfection as a predetermined destination that you must strive to reach, if you were to no longer make that real in any way, what could you start to choose with your body that you have not yet been choosing?

I often find it surprising how, even the very people who are most willing to have a life beyond the right, wrong, good, bad, and all the other rules and regulations of this world, still struggle to fit into this world. On the one hand, they may acknowledge how limited the various points of view they've been given are. But, on the other hand, they'd still like to be able to fit into that smaller dress or pant size.

People have determined and decided which social groups they belong to and do whatever they can to make sure they don't stand out from those groups, whether that is in their belief systems or their weight. Sometimes the social group that people put themselves in is that of the "outsider" or, the person with no social group. It's all still a game of categorization.

Body, what gift are you?

QUESTIONS TO PLAY WITH

What do you know?
What would you like to choose?

Have you decided that you "fit in" or "fit out"? And how are you measuring and determining that?

How much energy are you using to measure yourself into the standards of this world? How much energy are you using to measure out of the standards of this world? Are you, in any way using your body to measure in or out of the standards of this world? Do the measurements you use determine your value? If there was no "right" or "wrong", would you even have to measure?

Does having a body that looks a certain way make you more or less valuable, more or less lovable? What if you could go ahead and begin to love your body for the gift that it is, no matter what its shape, size, or weight is?

How Are You Using Your Weight?

What if you could actually live a life of ease, joy, and glory? Would you be willing to stand out from the crowd as the happy, joyful creature you can truly be? Or are you holding onto pains and problems that just won't "let you" be happy?

What are those pesky things that distract you from simply enjoying the gift that living can be? What is it you have decided you have to overcome before you can have ease? Have you put that burden on your body?

Are there any ways that you are using your weight to have a problem? Because we all know "everyone has problems." Weight is a very popular problem. Problems are a wonderful way to distract yourself.

Have you been using the problem of your body as a way to not be present with something else, some other possibility, or awareness? What questions could you ask to discover more of what's really going on for you? Is there anything that you are hiding or avoiding with your weight?

In my work facilitating people and their bodies, a very interesting point of view has come up around the topic of changing people's relationship to weight. Basically, people have shared the sense that others will not be able to handle them if their weight isn't an issue anymore. It is as though it is almost forbidden to let go of both the weight and the weight issue.

How is that for you? Are you forbidden to actually be happy with your body? Is there any energy in your world of "It is forbidden to love myself despite the weight, shape, and form of my body?"

If yes, what if you simply don't have to buy that anymore?

Everywhere you got the message from your family, or your ballet teacher, or your school, or friends, or wherever, that you can't like yourself if you look a certain way, would you be willing to let that go? What if those points of view and ways to relate to people just don't have to be your problem anymore?

What if "people won't be able to handle me if I don't have a weight thing" didn't have to be at all real in your world? All too frequently I see that as something people use to keep their connections with others. For example, I recently had a client tell me that her body size allows her to hang out with her friends' boyfriends without being perceived as a threat in any way.

Are you at all creating your body so that people are not threatened or intimidated by you?

How much are you using weight so that people can handle you?

Are you willing to be unhandle-able?

"Oh! Jennifer is amazing. I love her. She is so kind and sweet and fun. But she's a bit chubby so now I can handle her a bit more."

"Oh, Elise is amazing. Have you seen all that she creates? Fantastic! She is a bit fat, though."

This is what you are giving people so that they can handle you. What about being outrageous? What about being out of control? What about being the unhandle-able, uncontrollable, beyond this reality, potent dragon creature that you truly can be?

Stop trying to make yourself controllable through the weight you're choosing.

If you're skinny, that's just a point of view. If you're fat, that's just a point of view.

What if you could let go of all the necessity of those points of view and start to enjoy whatever body you have right this second, without having to wait to achieve some far-off goal, and without having to hold onto any "body problems" to make everyone around you more comfortable?

And, while we're asking, are those people really comfortable anyway? Will the people who require you to tone yourself down actually be happy if you make yourself small enough for them not to be threatened? What if it didn't matter what they are demanding? What if you could just begin to enjoy your body and your life, have your own body and life, no matter what?

What would it take for all of us to approach our bodies in an entirely different way?

What would you like to choose with your body now?

QUESTIONS TO PLAY WITH

What do you know?
What would you like to choose?

What is it you have decided that you have to overcome before you can have ease with your weight, before you can accept it?

What is it that you've decided you have to overcome before you have the weight that you or your body desire?

Where are you using weight as "your thing" that you have to put energy into and that you have to focus on because once that is overcome, everything will get better?

What does it even mean to "overcome" your weight? It is like a mirage, where as you move, so does your destination. Is overcoming your weight something that is even possible?

If weight or your body in any way is "your thing", ask:

Is it your thing to distract yourself from simply being happy?

Is it your thing because it makes you handle-able?

Is it your thing to make other people feel better?

Does it allow you to have a problem, just like everyone else?

What if it didn't have to be a thing at all? Then, what would your life be like?

The Mirror

What do you see when you look in the mirror? How much have you learned to see yourself through the eyes of judgment?

What is actually there when you look in the mirror? What is there that goes beyond the judgments? Again, judgments are simply points of view. They are not the absolute truth and they are not the only lens through which you can perceive your body.

The societies we live in are very much based on judgment. Everywhere you think you are seeing your body, but you are only seeing the judgments of your body, is where you are keeping yourself trapped in all that society has decided is right, wrong, good, bad, or what is supposed to be or not supposed to be.

Unfortunately, we have all learned to see ourselves through the eyes of judgment. But, what else is really possible? Where are you making the judgments you have of your body, the judgments other people have of their bodies, and the judgments other people have of your body more true than your choice to create your body? Would you be willing to be aware of all of those judgments and still know and receive the gift that your body is and can be?

What would it take for you to shed every filter and veil through which you see your body? What if you could see your body through the eyes of non-judgment, through the eyes of caring, kindness, and gratitude?

And, again, what if you don't have to do what everybody else is doing with their bodies? What if judgment was not the first thing you go to. What if, rather than immediately defining your "flaws", you could ask your body what it is showing you, so that when you see your stomach or any other body part, you don't immediately go to, "It's too fat." Instead you say, "Hey stomach. What's up? What's going on? What are you showing me? What can we create together?"

You may begin to notice that there are all sorts of things that we have learned we are supposed to desire with our bodies. We're supposed to want a flat stomach or a certain breast or butt size. But, have you ever taken a moment to get to know what it is that you actually desire?

What do you think you desire, that you don't even desire, that you don't wonder if you desire it, that keeps you in the lie that you desire it? Or, more simply, what is it you truly desire with your body? And, more than anything else, what does your body desire?

I mean, truly, what we've learned to desire may not have anything to do with what would actually be fun for us. If you go to India or to Africa, and you are skinny, people think you're sick. They'll tell you, "You're not eating enough!" And they will want to stuff your face, because you should be a bit chubby. Being chubby is when you're happy. Being chubby is when you're rich. When you're skinny, you're poor and pathetic.

In the west, you have to be skinny to be beautiful. And if you're a bit more than skinny, you're fat. Even a little bit of fat is too much. Skinny, chubby, fat: it's all full of judgment. If you were actually able to get to a place where nothing was right or wrong, or true or false, what could you be aware of? What does your body desire to look like?

Do you dare to ask that question? Or do you not trust

that your body could actually tell you what it desires? Or, even more, that knowing and creating with your body could actually be joyful for you?

Body, what new joys and adventures are available today?

QUESTIONS TO PLAY WITH

What do you know?
What would you like to choose?

Take a moment and look at yourself in the mirror.

What do you see?

What feelings come up when you look at yourself in the mirror?

Do you use any of those feelings to prove that you or your body are messed up in any way?

Where do your eyes go?

Do you immediately notice all of the supposed flaws you have decided are wrong about your body?

If yes, be present with all of the energies that come up.

Did any of those judgments originate with you, or did they come from other people?

How many judgments are you "wearing" for other

people?

And would you still like to, or can you let any of them go now?

What if you could see your body through the eyes of someone who cares about and adores you?

Would you be so bold as to be that caring and adoring of you?

Would you be willing to see the parts of your body that you adore such as the colour of your skin, the shape of your ears, or the joy in your smile?

Are there any ways that you have been taking the miracle of your body for granted, and instead favouring the drama of the judgments about your body?

And, what if ALL of that is okay? Whatever you choose, whether it's gratitude or judgment, is all just a choice.

Anywhere that you notice judgments, just take a moment to be with them. Notice the energy they create, and how those energies resonate in your body.

Notice the energy that any bit of gratitude and/or appreciation for your body creates.

How does that resonate in your body?

Which energies would you like to invite into living with your body?

Beyond all sense of right and wrong or should and should not, what if you could simply choose to play with whichever energies you would like to play with?

When you notice judgments, you don't have to buy them. You can simply be present with them and know that you have the freedom to hold onto them or to let them go.

What if looking in a mirror could be a chance for you to see something wildly unique and miraculous today?

(After all, there has never been another YOU before.)

Who Are You Creating Your Body For?

I was once speaking with a woman who told me of something she had recently become aware of with her body. Her father liked women to be a little chubby. Though her mother and father were still married, her mother was not really available to her father as his wife any longer. So, this woman had begun to form her body in a way that her father liked, to be that for him.

Isn't that amazing?!

What body form are you using to please the people in your life? What are the needs you are aware of in other people's worlds? Are you trying to fulfil other people's supposed needs through the body size they require and desire, instead of looking at what you require and desire?

Other people have reported being brought up in a home where their mothers were extremely physically competitive with them, constantly comparing their bodies and judging who was the most attractive. I have known women to turn down the sexual energies of their bodies so as to make their mothers more comfortable. This is just the tip of the iceberg with the ways that we will actually create our bodies for the people around us.

Are you, in any way, making yourself desirable to somebody that you don't even desire to have that relationship with? And even if you would desire that relationship, what if you didn't have to adjust your body shape, size, or form? Are you turning down the possibilities for your body to please someone else?

QUESTIONS TO PLAY WITH

What do you know?
What would you like to choose?

Where are you pleasing either or both of your parents with the body form you are choosing?

Where are you pleasing your friends or society with the body form you are choosing?

And, at the end of the day, are they even pleased with what you are choosing?!

Who are you replacing with the body you are choosing?

Have you stepped into the role of mother, father, aunt, uncle, grandma, grandpa, lover, friend, or confidante?

What are you being for everybody while being nothing for yourself?

What jobs have you taken on that do not need to be yours?

Could you fire yourself from any role that you've taken on?

Would you allow yourself to let go of any and all body forms, shapes, or sizes that you have been choosing to match what other people desire, instead of being who you would like to be?

Who are you being, that if you didn't have to be them, could allow you to be you?

Hiding

Take a moment and get present with anywhere that you may be desiring to hide. Are you using your weight, your body shape, or your size to hide? And how much energy are you using to make yourself hidden? Where are you hiding away from the world by using the judgments of the world?

All too often we think that we must hide because we have decided there is something not quite right about us. We hide what is most different about us. But, what if that difference is a brilliant gift that we are withholding from everyone?

What if you have been spending all this energy judging and holding back the magnificence of you and your body that the world is longing for?

Truly, what have you decided to hide as though it is so wrong, bad, terrible, and awful about you that is actually the brilliance of you that could lighten up the world?

When you get lost in the right and wrong of you, all you are doing is giving your energy to judgment. Each different person could come up with a different judgment. There is no ultimate right or wrong that everyone agrees upon. Ultimately, judgment is simply an invention that society has come up with to determine what people should or should not choose. You buying into those judgments does nothing more than make you a supporter of the very society that is limiting you.

Beyond that, when you hide yourself through your weight, shape, and size while simultaneously loading it with the energy of judgment, it makes you really visible! The judgments become like neon signs that invite even more judgments.

So, ask yourself, how much energy are you using to hide away from you? How much energy are you using to hide away from the life that you would actually like to create? For example, if you judge yourself as too fat, or too tall, or too ugly, do you allow yourself to get up on stage and sing like you may have always wanted to? Do you allow yourself to engage with all of the people that you might like to? Or do you use your body as a reason and justification to not choose what might actually bring more joy into your world?

This is a big, sneaky one! After all, when you choose to hide something about yourself, you may begin to hide it even from yourself.

So, let's dive deeper.

QUESTIONS TO PLAY WITH

What do you know?
What would you like to choose?

Is there anywhere that you are using your body to hide your brilliance from you so that you cannot access it? If there were nothing to hide, what would you create with your body? What might you discover? What is truly available now if you start choosing you - the brilliance of you, the genius of you, and the magnificence of you?

What light have you kept dim or even turned off that you can now allow to really turn on and let glow? Let yourself be that beacon of light. Let your body be that possibility of joyful embodiment that is available to you if you would simply choose it.

For a moment, I would like you to tap into when you were 2 hours old. Recall the energy that you and your body were being. What were you aware of as a possibility with your body? What joy was available to you then? What discoveries did you have with your body? What exploration of wiggling toes, and sounds, and smells, and miraculous possibilities were available to you then? What choices did you make to be with this body and this life? And what would it take for you to choose right now to have even greater clarity, awareness, and presence with your body and this life you are creating?

Would you be willing to make the choice to stop hiding and to explore what else is possible for you with this body?

Does Your Body Need to Change?

What if you're actually okay the way you are?

What if you don't have to lose weight?

What if you don't have to change your shape or size?

What if there is nothing wrong with you?

Would you even know what to do with yourself if you didn't have anything to judge about you anymore?

I was speaking to some clients about this and it blew their minds.

"What?!" they said. "Of course I have to lose weight because of my health issues."

Okay. But what if that is not exactly how it has to be?

Where have you decided two things are causally related that might not be? What if it is the energy of the decisions, conclusions, and judgments you are holding onto that is impacting your body and your world? Have you decided that your weight is connected to your health, and if you don't lose weight, your health issues won't change? Where might that be keeping both of those issues alive?

Many, many people have been told by their doctors and the medical world that weight makes them wrong and is the cause of many problems. But, what if that is not exactly how it will occur for each and every one of you? Have you jumped to any conclusions about your health? Have you created any causality between weight and health that is not actually true for you and your body?

Now, I get that this may go against much of how you have been viewing your body. What I am asking is for you to ask these questions for your own awareness. Allow yourself to notice everything that comes up when you ask these questions: the irritations, the confusion, the happiness, or whatever. Any energies that you become aware of that do not make your life more joyful, simply relax around and let go of. This does not mean ignoring the cues that your body is giving you. It is simply a chance for you to let go of the charge around all of it. After all, what's the value of having weight that you are not happy with, health difficulties, and being generally bummed out?

What if you were to start to let go of the energetic tension around all of this?

Would that contribute to your enjoyment of your body?

Would you be willing to let go of all the feelings that there is something wrong with you and move on from there, into creating with your awareness whatever would bring the most joy to your world…right away?

Living and Dying

Throughout the years that I have worked with people, I have discovered often the seemingly most bizarre questions can get right to the heart of what is actually going on. The key to being able to work with the information that arises is to choose to let go of any and all judgment. Judgment does not create. Judgment destroys possibilities and all awareness that don't match that particular judgment.

If you would like to discover the unexpected energies, choices, and decisions you may be using to create your body and your life, remember to acknowledge and then simply set any and all judgments aside. As with all of the questions that we have been exploring in this book, allowing your mind to relax and letting your body and your energetic awareness take charge can give you a totally different sense of what is going on for you.

And so we come to the subject of living and dying.

What are the choices you have made for living and for dying, with and through your body? Would you be willing to take a vulnerable look into this somewhat taboo subject?

Are there any ways that you have been using your body to measure your right to be here? Is there anywhere you are measuring yourself so that you can be sure to be right, so that you have permission to live? Or, is there anywhere that you have already determined and decided that you just don't fit in, and you don't even like this world, so you will just say screw you to everything by dying?

Where are you not allowing yourself to live because the standards of this world don't work for you?

Do you actually desire to live?

If that's a no, what ease, joy, and glory can you choose to be aware of all that, and to create from where you truly ARE, rather than where you think you are "supposed to" be, with the answers that you are "supposed to" have? If you are functioning from the energetic point of view of "this world is such a pain and the only way to deal with it seems to be to leave it or to avoid it", let yourself acknowledge that is what is going on for you. You cannot change what you keep hidden from yourself.

If you start to really live from asking questions, rather than coming to conclusions, how much would you have a choice to live or to die? What if, after all, death is just death? It's just a choice. Not a bad thing. Not a good thing. It's just one possibility of many.

Have you been allowing your judgments and your conclusions to limit your awareness of what else is actually possible for you?

Is there anywhere that you are not allowing yourself to enjoy the creation of living with your body that is actually possible for you? Is there anywhere that you are using your body to destroy rather than to create? Have you, at all, seen your body as an unconscious thing that you must destroy?

Have you been using your weight to "weigh yourself out" of life and living? What choices are available for you to no longer have to measure yourself, or use your weight to destroy you anymore?

If you started to ask your body more questions, how much would you actually eat? Where are you stuffing your body or depriving your body to take you to the death that you have decided is your one and only choice in this world?

What if that were not true?! What if there are so many choices you simply have not yet explored? Would you be willing to use both your creative and your destructive capacities in a different way? Where are you killing possibilities when you could be killing lies, limitations, and judgments? What would you like to choose now?

Now What?

Here you are. Armed with a lot of questions, you have embarked on this journey of creation with your body.

What interesting, unexpected discoveries have you made? Have you noticed any changes? Have you gone through these questions, looking for the right, good, and perfect answers? Have you noticed any releasing of judgments? Wherever you are right now, know that this adventure of embodiment is yours to create.

The questions and discussions in this book endeavour to be an invitation for you to take the energies you have been using to judge and condemn you and your body, and direct all of that mojo toward exploring what would be fun for you, what would be delicious for you, and what would bring an ever-growing smile to your face.

Thank you for being courageous enough to step off the beaten path of the right and wrong of having a body. Your choice to be different in any and all of the ways you choose can be a source of possibilities for others in the world to choose the path that works for them. What a gift!

Now, get out there and enjoy your body.

I dare you to.

Wanting More?

This book could not have come into being without the great gift and resource that is Access Consciousness®. Throughout the years, Access Consciousness has sought to empower people to "know that they know."

Approaching all of life from the questions of "What else is possible?" and "How does it get better than this?" has led people across the globe to shift all areas of their lives in ways that actually bring them ease, joy, and glory (an exuberant expression of abundance).

If this book has inspired you to look for something greater, or you have just always known something else must be possible, know that there is an enormous space available, full of tools and techniques to explore your knowledge of yourself and the world around you. Head over to the Access Consciousness website to find more books, videos, classes, and facilitators worldwide at www.accessconsciousness.com

Just watch out. You could get incredibly happy.

About the Author

Kalpana Raghuraman was born in the Netherlands to South-Indian parents, who nurtured her to be curious about 'the universe' and human potential. These years as a child really set the ground work that allowed her to be, and to this day remain, curious about that which goes beyond, and a seeker of more than what this world says is possible. She knows consciousness is powerful and magical and always contributing to those who are willing to receive.

Having learned Bharatanatyam (classical south-Indian dance) from her mother who was one of the first to run a dance school in the Netherlands, Kalpana has always had an affinity with bodies. Access Consciousness® gave her access to clarity with her own capacities and awareness with bodies. As a 3-Day Body Class facilitator and choreographer, she is able to share many of these talents with the world. The struggle with body shape, form, and size is something she encountered a lot in the dance field as well as with participants in her classes. With *You & Your Body* she hopes to create more awareness, more clarity, more peace, and definitely more joy for people with their bodies.

Kalpana is an Access Consciousness Certified Facilitator with a global business that takes her across the globe, and also choreographer and artistic director of her dance company Kalpanarts. For more information about Kalpana and her work visit:

Website: kalpanaraghuraman.com
Facebook: @kalpana.raghuraman
Instagram: @kalpana_raghuraman

www.ingramcontent.com/pod-product-compliance
Lightning Source LLC
Chambersburg PA
CBHW010742170426
43193CB00018BA/2917